Blood, Sweat and Careers

......Six Steps to Exceptional Career
Performance

Angela Cahill

First Published in 2009 by

The Chancery Coaching Company
107-111 Fleet Street
London
EC4A 2AB

Printed by Philtone Litho Limited, Bristol, BS5 7EY

Design by www.afishinsea.co.uk

Photography by www.garnhamphotography.co.uk

Typeset in Tahoma

Order now at www.bloodsweatandcareers.com

ISBN: 978 0 9563125 0 1

Contents

Acknowledgements   2

Introduction   4

......Six Steps to Exceptional Career Performance

Step 1 – Assess Your Potential   8

The Principles of Success   11
Cards on the Table   17
Your Offering   23
Skills Analysis   26
What motivates you...   33

Step 2 – Plan Your Route   38

What's your passion?   42
Thinking BIGG   48
Goal Setting for Success   50
The Sap Success Model   60
Mind Control through NLP   64

Step 3 – Gather Your "A" Team   72

How do you choose your Team?   75
What parties do you go to?   76
Networking to Win   77
I have my team, what next?   78

Step **4** **– Dig for Opportunities** 80

Job Search Techniques – Fact V Fiction 83
The Hidden Opportunities on the Net! 84
Working with Recruiters 86
Making speculative applications 89

Step **5** **– Create A Winning Pitch** 92

Writing a Phenomenal CV 94
A Winning Letter of Application! 106
The truth about Interviews... 110
Interview Questions 114
Interview Checklist 120

Step **6** **– Evaluate and Refocus** 122

How to evaluate a Job Offer 126
Get some feedback! 130
Exceptional Career Performance 136
Rewards V Consequences 140
28 days Later 142

What now? 146

About the Author 152

Acknowledgements

I will try and thank all the wonderful people who helped me create this book and build my experience but if I have forgotten anyone, I thank you now!

Thank you to my wonderful, happy and positive family for your continued encouragement, for putting up with me (far from easy!) and being a welcome sounding board to all my ideas throughout my careers - in Marketing, as a Headhunter and now as a Corporate & Career Coach. I enjoy a very happy life and that's down to you.

Thank you to Sam Fulljames who I dedicate this book to. You are 'one in a million' with incredible qualities and have helped me in so many ways of which I'm truly grateful. Thank you also to all The Fulljames Family for always believing in me. I couldn't have achieved my dreams without you.

Thank you to the exceptional people at Blue Legal. Each and every one of you have restored my faith in the Recruitment and Headhunting Industry. You prove beyond a shadow of a doubt that the job can be done by people who care deeply about creating happy solutions all round. You are the best of the best and have been a pleasure to work with in all capacities.

Thank you to the beautiful Carmen Spence, my executive assistant, for your inner wisdom and invaluable help in putting together my ideas and thoughts to create this book.

Thank you to the most inspiring people I have met in my life. I can't mention them all but would like to mention Paula Coates, Jon Scott, Emma Ronaghan, Giles Daniels, Brett, Mark Harris, Scarlette, Michael B, Hayley & Michael Ormrod, Ryan, Barbara & Grayson Elliott, Libby, Sonia Cleary, Stephen T, Rob, Kate & Maya Ogilvy. Last but not least thanks to Nigel, where would I be without you?

"The greatest gift that God can give us is to see ourselves as others see us"

Nancy Cahill
(How great thou art)

Introduction

So you have opened up this book and that's a great start. I take it you want to achieve phenomenal success in your working life?

The Question is "Are you serious?"

I'm going to give you 6 assurances!

- If you have a strong desire to achieve, you will
- If you are prepared to put the work in, you will make it
- There are people out there that want you to succeed
- It is totally your decision what happens now
- You have nothing to lose by engaging in these steps
- If you start today, you will get to your destination sooner

This is your life and no one can live it for you.

But it's your decision now.

Most of the readers will do what they always do...start reading and give up halfway through.

Is this you?

Or is today different?

I have enjoyed a varied career and been very fortunate to achieve what I consider to be phenomenal success. I know that drive has a lot to do with it. But it doesn't stop there.

Anyone can do it, it's no big deal. And I mean **ANYONE** can do it. Anyone prepared to take massive action and start today!

Most of my career has been working as an owner and MD of a Headhunting and Executive Recruitment Business which lead me to Corporate and Career Coaching. I have met over 3000 people in the last 12 years - all looking to reach their potential.

Looking back I am overwhelmed by the challenge that they think they face...that's right I said *think* they face. The same issues arise time and time again with personal development and career development. I've spent the last two years examining people very closely, taking extensive notes and was intrigued and inspired to examine exactly what you need to do to achieve phenomenal success in your career.

I did it myself, I enjoyed studying successful people and feel it's time to share these ideas with others, hence my reason to write this book.

I know some of you will think I had it easy but I didn't.

Let's be really honest - It's not an easy road for any woman in the city. All the talk about the "glass ceiling" and that we live in a "man's world" isn't just talk. I came across lots of problems along the way which I'll share with you as we go along. However there is equally discrimination against all sorts of people.

The world of work isn't full of equal opportunities now is it?

I have witnessed at all levels of recruitment and promotion:

- The continual discrimination against race/sex/disability/age.
- The common snobbery about a candidate's background and even their schooling!
- The qualifications they may not have (but quite seriously do not need!)
- The fear of employing people of a different culture and/or religion

But much more importantly than this, some people succeed over others because:

- They know how to "play the game"

.....and it is a game.

Call it a game of life, success game, career game, whatever you want but the fact is some people play it better than others.

This is the **only thing that is in your control**. This is what I have researched and why I have put together the **Six Steps** I know will lead you to the finishing line.

It pains me to say that this book isn't for everyone... but it isn't. There are many people out there who are "happy with their lot" and don't think they want (or deserve) a better today or tomorrow.

I guess you are reading this book because there is some part of you that knows you have yet to be the best you can be! That's a great start!

For this to be a worthwhile exercise for you, I need just three assurances from you now:

1. Have a completely **open mind** and **engage** with the exercises

2. **Write in the book**! Don't make the mistake of thinking you need to keep it clean. You can keep it at home so no one needs to know your personal thoughts. Unless you want them to.

3. **Start TODAY!**

Good luck.

Blood, Sweat and Careers

......**Six Steps** to Exceptional Career
Performance

Step 1

— Assess Your Potential

"The difference between the impossible and the possible lies in a man's determination."

Tommy Lasorda

Assess Your Potential

When I started my first company at 26, I looked for a mentor and coach to help the business reach it's potential. And I found him.

But I didn't like for one minute his opening line...

He said "The first and most important thing you need to know Angela is to work on **yourself** harder than on your business!"

To be honest I wondered what I was paying him for. Surely his job was to talk through my new ideas and my strategy and therefore to maximise my company's profit? I always say it's lonely at the top and its invaluable to have a guide. Here I was paying him a lot of money and bouncing my business ideas off this guy only for him to tell me to self examine, set personal as well as business goals and to find balance and control. "If you get your own house in order, watch your business follow" he said.

I wasn't buying any of it.

It was a good 3 years later, after working very closely with Senior Executives, Chief Executives and CEO's that I started noticing the clear trend. I stumbled across people who had seen enormous success. I witnessed people going from zero to hero. Yes I started to notice what these people had something in common.

There are keys to building a successful life and a successful career. There are ways you can identify and build on your strengths, your skills, your motivations and your career aspirations and gain phenomenal success. There are ways you can build on your current situation and master the secret to success.

The Principles of Success

Are you reading this hoping to hear age old (tired) theories? Are you waiting for me to regurgitate the business guru's who have written many books on the "Masters of Success"?

I hope not. I am only going to give you the truth about my research findings. Controversial or not.

I was giving a keynote speech this month when I asked the room to put their hands up if this question applied to them...."Who likes winning?...raise your hand!" and secondly "Who likes losing?...raise your hand!" What do you think happened?

No one raised their hand to the last question.

So if everyone likes winning, why is it that only some people achieve success? I would say it's because my question that I asked should have been more akin to:

"Which of you has an overriding passion and **DESIRE** to win?"

"Who will do want it takes to win?"

"Who will do what they need to succeed?"

"The starting point of all achievement is desire. Keep this constantly in mind. Weak desire brings weak results, just as a small amount of fire makes a small amount of heat."

Napoleon Hill

Conducting the research for this book was enlightening.

I have really enjoyed studying many successful people in business. Successful people are not always the people with the top grades, quality background or experience. Don't take my word for it; consider the people in the public eye:

- Richard Branson left school at the age of 15
- Alan Sugar left at 16!
- Walt Disney was fired by a newspaper editor for lack of ideas and went bankrupt several times before the wonderful world of Disneyland
- In Charles Darwin's autobiography he wrote "I was considered by all my masters and by my father, a very ordinary boy, rather below the common standard of intellect."
- Duncan Bannatyne OBE, after his naval career (which included a spell in military prison) expanded his career from ice cream van vendor to one of the most successful and respected businessmen in the UK
- Chris Gardner (brought to life by Will Smith in the Film the Pursuit of Happiness) went from no job, no home and no money to a multi millionaire with his own brokerage firm in Chicago.

So what is their secret? How did they do it?

And how did they get over those obstacles I talked about that you see in business. You know the way that people are discriminated against...due to education/experience/background etc? It never made a dot of difference to these people.

"If you think you can, or think you can't
you're probably right"

Henry Ford

What's the difference between them and you?

There are **SIX** qualities that successful people have:

1. **They believe THEY CAN do it and they believe they deserve it**
2. **They have a dream, a vision and desire**
3. **They have a PLAN and set GOALS**
4. **They have (and/or are willingly to gain) the skills to succeed in their chosen career/business**
5. **They are willing to work hard and work within a mastermind team**
6. **They never give up**

Does this sound like you? If it doesn't already this is what you need to embrace to get to success.

But how is success measured in the business world? (WARNING: you may not like this....)

Success in Business is only ever measured in Financial Terms

Like it or not. It's a fact and you can dress it up with "reaching CEO", "getting acknowledged", "achieving a promotion/pay rise etc" it is viewed **by others** in financial terms...maybe not by you but certainly in our society.

However this is viewed is perhaps irrelevant. When you think of success, how do you picture it?

When I started working with The Chancery Coaching Company, we looked at the elements of life that are sometimes the root of unhappiness and posted some questions on our website. I thought you may like to see them, if only to get a reality check on what's going well or not well for you. I'd like you to complete the following quick and easy exercise to see where you are in your thinking.

Have a go!

1. Do you dream about where you want to be in life and think that it is so far out of your reach you may as well give up?
2. Do you yearn for a new job or career and don't know how to go about it?
3. Are you unhappy with the way you look?
4. Are you unhappy with your health, or your weight or the exercise you do but just don't know how to make any changes?
5. Are you in the right relationship – is it not working the way you would like or do you feel trapped?
6. Do you find yourself on your own too often or out with friends you don't want to be with or doing things you don't want to do?
7. Do you feel you have a poor quality of life? Or do you feel you have no time on your hands to do the things you enjoy?
8. Are you stressed about your finances and don't know how to make the changes to put things right?
9. Do you have habits that you would rather give up as they have a negative effect on your life?
10. Are you worried and does this often keep you awake at night?

Does this sound like you...or you may want to simply inject more success into your life. And why not? Why waste valuable time having that feeling that something isn't quite right and you could be happier and more successful?

Cards on the Table

Have you ever heard of "The wheel of life"? If you have done one of these in the past, do go for it again - this is a great exercise to start off some self examination.   It's a simple exercise, have a go!

The Wheel of Life is divided into eight segments each of which is determined by the areas of your life that impact you as a person and your ultimate success. These sectors can be for example, family, friends, career, partner, me time, sports or exercise, hobbies etc.

So this is what I would like you to do:

1. Write in the segments of the wheel the eight most important areas of your life (wheel provided below)
2. Score each area out of 10 and mark from 1-10 on the spokes of the wheel your level of satisfaction in that area of your life (1 being the least satisfied and 10 most satisfied).
3. Connect the dots around your wheel – here's an example...

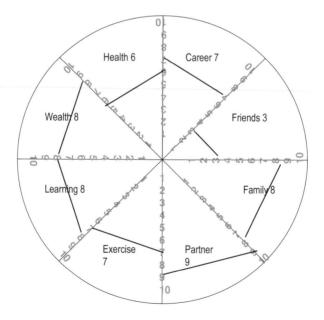

Now it's your turn...

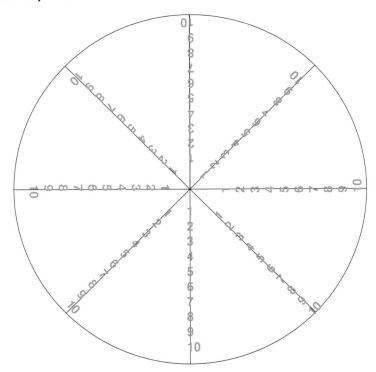

Once you have completed this wheel balancing chart, then ask yourself the following questions:

1 - Which area of my life was my lowest score?
2 - Which are of my life was my highest score?
3 - Would my wheel travel smoothly on the ground or am I in for a bumpy ride?
4 - Which areas do I want to work on to develop my goals?
5 - What can I personally do to improve things?
6 - What can I ask others to do?
7 - How much do I really want to improve these areas?
8 – What five action points can I set myself to do THIS WEEK?

Now let's look about your career wheel. If you are searching for career success it's all too easy to believe that you are unhappy in your job so you should go to another company. However it could be something to do with your current role – say the work, the level, the pay and the future possibilities. Therefore let's examine where you are in your career before we go on to assessing your skills.

So tell me how you would rank the following elements. Please add/amend any elements as appropriate for you.

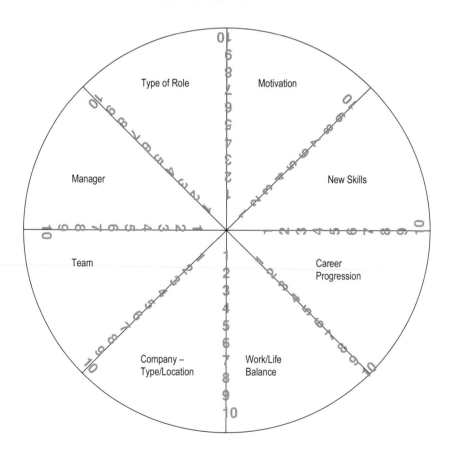

Now ask yourself:

1 - Which area of my career was my lowest score?

2 - Which are of my career was my highest score?

3 - Would my wheel travel smoothly on the ground or am I in for a bumpy ride?

4 - Which areas do I want to work on to develop my goals?

5 - What can I personally do to improve things?

6 - What can I ask others to do?

7 - How much do I really want to improve these areas?

8 – What five action points can I set myself to do THIS WEEK?

Out of interest, how easy is it to answer the following questions?

What makes you unique?

What makes you special?

Now fast forward, imagine you are in the autumn of your life and looking back over your career history. Complete the following sentences:

I wish I had been:

I am most proud of:

I wish I had done more of:

This process of self examination is essential to get you to understand where you want to get to, what skills you have and what you can offer.

"Analysing what you haven't got as well as what you have is a necessary ingredient of a career."

Orison Swett Marden

Your Offering

Let's start with the basics. Let's see what skills you have gained along the road so far.

I wonder how good you are at examining your key strengths and weaknesses. In the table below please have a go at listing your strengths and weaknesses. The process of writing this down helps you to really think about what you consider to be your strengths and weaknesses – what separates you from someone else and which areas you need to work on to improve. Be true to yourself and take time to think of all possibilities!

Strengths	Weaknesses

Now have a look at the strengths and weaknesses in the table below. Please tick which apply to you. Maybe you haven't thought about any of these!

One of your Strengths	✓	A potential Weakness	✓
Inspiring		Augmentative	
Ambitious		Loner	
Reliable		Confrontational	
Independent		Procrastinator	
Detail Conscious		De-motivated	
Great attitude		Unreliable	
Dedicated/Committed		No common sense	
Networked		Not enough experience	
Motivated		Poorly Presented	
Loves a challenge		Lazy/Lethargic	
Can delegate		No Time management	
Good organisational skills		Procrastination	
Multi-tasking Abilities		Plodder	
Trustworthy		No ambition	
Creative		Unenthusiastic	
Sense of Humour		Nervous	
Management		Tardy	
Organised		Unsociable	
Avoids Conflict ***		Avoids Conflict ***	
Quick to Act ***		Quick to Act ***	
Perfectionist ***		Perfectionist ***	
Confidence ***		Confidence ***	

Did any of this surprise you?

Did it add to your skill base?

Notice the last four could be seen as strengths or weaknesses.

Now you are ready to chart yourself with the use of a SWOT analysis. This will help you to take into account your current situation and your desired situation and all those obstacles that may get in the way of your perfect career plan.

Please prepare your personal SWOT:

Personal SWOT Analysis

Key Strengths	Weaknesses To Improve
Opportunities for Career Growth	Threats to my Growth

What action are you prepared to take to combat any negative factors and capitalise on the positives?

Skills Analysis

The next step is to look at what actual skills you have, which of these you actually enjoy and which ones you want to develop.

If any of these I have listed have no bearing on your current work situation or future career, just pass right by them.

For the skills that do relate to you, rate your level of proficiency here from Beginner (1) to Expert (5).

You may wish to ask for help on this exercise or go through it with a friend who knows your work life well or even a trusted colleague.

Exercise – Skills Analysis – Part One:

Communication & Interpersonal Skills

Specific Skill:	Competency Beginner - Expert 1 2 3 4 5	Do I enjoy it?	Do I wish to develop this skill?
Self Awareness			
Personal Development			
Work Life Balance			
Time Management			
Setting Boundaries			
Strong Verbal Communication			
Strong Written Communication Skills			
Empathising with Others			
Motivating Others			
Leading Others			
Engaging Others			

Representing Others			
Good Listening Skills			
Putting People at Ease			
Building durable relationships			
Setting personal Goals and Objectives			
Goal Setting for Others			
Recruiting the right people			
Facilitating			
Decision Making			
Interviewing Skills			
Chairing Meetings			
Influencing/Persuading Others			
Negotiation Skills			
Speaking/Presenting			
Giving & receiving feedback			
Mediating, Resolving conflict			
Foreign Languages			
Other:			
Other:			
Other:			
Other:			

Exercise – Skills Analysis – Part Two:

Business Development and Strategy Skills

Specific Skill:	Competency Beginner - Expert 1 2 3 4 5	Do I enjoy it?	Do I wish to develop this skill?
Business Strategy & Planning			
Preparing Winning Business Plans			
Making Effective Business Decisions			
Business Growth			
Profit Focus			
Pitching for Business			
Winning Pitches			
Investigative/Research Skills			
Planning Tasks and Projects			
Ability to Interpret Financial Data			
Lateral Thinking			
Developing the ideas of others			
Seeing the Big Picture			
Competitive Analysis			
Resource Allocation			
Strong Sales Skills			
Problem Solving Ability			

Time Saving Initiatives			
Working Under Pressure			
Marketing of products and services			
Producing effective market research			
Writing clear and effective Marketing Messages			
Other:			
Other:			
Other:			
Other:			

Exercise – Skills Analysis – Part Three:

Management and Finance Skills

Specific Skill:	Competency Beginner - Expert 1 2 3 4 5	Do I enjoy it?	Do I wish to develop this skill?
Building Effective Teams			
Coaching and Motivating Others			
Delegating Effectively			
Retaining Talented Employees			
Performance Management			
Day to Day Management of Others			
Succession Planning			
Leadership			
Effective Administration			
Managing the Workflow			
Change Management			
Training Others			
Facilitating Group Discussion			
Creating new systems and procedures			
Managing customers, internal and/or external			
Critical Assessment about business issues			

Networking			
Brainstorming			
Managing a diverse workforce			
Managing a virtual or remote team			
Regularly Reaching Team Targets			
Business Planning			
Budgeting and Forecasting			
Analysing financial information			
Cash Flow Projections			
Understanding of the bottom line			
Risk Assessment			
Analysing Data			
Systems Management			
Analysing financial information			
Cost Accounting			
Other:			
Other:			
Other:			
Other:			

Exercise – Skills Analysis – Part Four:

Information Technology Skills

Specific Skill:	Competency Beginner - Expert 1 2 3 4 5	Do I enjoy it?	Do I wish to develop this skill?
Microsoft Office Applications			
Spreadsheet Manipulation			
Project Management through IT Applications			
Presentation Software e.g. PowerPoint			
Website Development			
Content Management			
Graphics			
Specific Software for your particular career:			
1 -			
2 -			
3 -			
Using the Internet for Research			
Other:			
Other:			
Other:			
Other:			

What motivates you?

Motivation is key to success and the process of establishing what motivates you makes for a wonderful path for change.

As a Headhunter I have come across various candidates at different stages of their career and when I meet someone with a positive attitude, they will find the motivation to do exceptionally well. On the other hand, when I meet someone who is lethargic, beaten or who feels sorry for themselves, they will never find the motivation to achieve their goals. I can see it every time.

You only get the motivation for doing something when you start doing it. That's for sure. You have to be on the right path to get started so tell me:

What motivates you? Ask yourself:

- What will be the ideal type of work or career for me? ***Think about times that you have been so absorbed in what you were doing that you lost track of time or sat with a friend or colleague and got excited about their role?
- What seems to make me most fulfilled and excited? ***Work related or not...try and think of times when you've been working on a personal or work project. Which stages of a project drive you the most – the planning, the implementing, the close?
- What work should I stay away from and why?
- What about myself do I have trouble seeing?
- What aspects of myself do I need to change to be more successful and motivated?
- What aspects of myself should I harness?

Let's look at what you enjoy...

This easy exercise always provides real insight about a job or work environment that you like – or don't like.

By writing down anything about your job, your work environment, the culture, the hours, the way of working etc – you will be able to see what rewards you are seeking at work and therefore what your core career focus should be. Get creative. Perhaps you want to write down "I want to be home at 5pm and don't like working late" or "I don't like working alone and need to work with others" or "I don't like working indoors"

Have a go…and come back to this exercise when your career starts changing…

What I like	What I dislike

If you have completed these exercises (and if you haven't – go back a step!) then you should have a solid idea of what you like, what you don't like and what kind of position will provide instant motivation.

But what matters most at work?

What do you actually need to be satisfied? What influences your Job Satisfaction?

Job Satisfiers	Level of importance or value				
	Low				High
	1	2	3	4	5
Authority and Power Decision Making, Management, Power and Influence within the Company					
Physical Environment The workspace is desirable. Right Location, Commutable, Work from Home					
Financial Status and Reward Stable Pay Structure, Benefits, Raises, Promotion Opportunities, Bonus etc					
Work Life Balance Ability to balance work and life demands and interests					
Recognition and Reward Recognition for the work you do and compensation through bonus/commission					
Affiliation Teamwork, Working with an intelligent peer group.					
Stimulation Interesting. Scope for Learning & Development					
Other:					

So what did you discover?

What are the most important aspects of Job Satisfaction for you?

What are the least important aspects of Job Satisfaction for you?

How well does your current job meet your needs?

Congratulations, you have completed the first step! You should now have figured out:

- ✓ The Principles of Success
- ✓ The areas of your life that are in and out of balance
- ✓ The areas of your career that you want to work on
- ✓ Your Strengths and Weaknesses
- ✓ The Opportunities and Threats to your Career Growth
- ✓ The Skills you have to offer, enjoy and wish to develop
- ✓ What motivates you
- ✓ The Key Job Satisfiers you are looking for

Well done!

Blood, Sweat and Careers

......**Six Steps** to Exceptional Career
Performance

Step 2

– Plan Your Route

"If you wish to achieve worthwhile things in your personal and career life, you must become a worthwhile person in your own self-development."

Brian Tracy

Plan Your Route

I am a big believer in goal setting and focus. I am not sure how anyone can get anywhere in life without having some goals and going in the right direction with the right attitude.

As I said earlier it is 100% evident in the qualities of all the successful people around the world. I am sure some of them don't write them down regularly, well not on paper, but those individuals usually have people within their businesses who write the basics while they consider the outcome.

When you're working out your route it's essential to consider what outcomes you would like to achieve. For this I believe structured planning starts nothing short of considering your real passion in life and thinking 'BIGG'! Then it takes setting SMART goals, following the SAP Success Model and using the power of Mind Control through NLP. But more of that later....

I good friend of mine always told me that the key to a successful working life is to:

"Chase your passion!
....not your pension"

When I did so my fortunes changed and my pension followed. I meet many people through coaching who have continued on a path that they never intended. They often think that because they are now in their late 30's, it is too late to change.

"What would you do if you
knew you couldn't fail?"

It is never too late to change. If you aren't getting the career satisfaction you always desired, if you are constantly thinking:

I've missed the boat...
I wish I had become a Teacher, a Vet, a Stockbroker, a Lawyer...
I wish I worked for Greenpeace (you get the drift)...
If only I didn't study law at University...
Someday I hope to start my own business...

The time for change is now.

What's your passion?

Good question and one where the answer may have been buried away inside you for years. Now is the time to unveil it and time for you to think about what you have always wanted. Do you know what it is that will make you happy? What do you want for your future? What do you want out of life?

Exercise - My Perfect Scenario

If I could do anything in the world I would...

Imagine for a moment that you have achieved this dream and you are right there watching it happen.

How do you feel?

What do you see?

Who is around you?

What would you next?

Successful entrepreneurs are always a joy to be around and really interesting creatures. What I have noticed is that their thinking is always focused on the end result. How they will feel when they get to their goals. They work to outcome theories where their aim is to consider the outcome of their goals and how this will make them feel.

By using the principles of what I call E-Thinking - the entrepreneur's way of thinking, I have noticed a key difference in their focusing tool.

Most people don't achieve their dreams because of their focus on problems and "what if scenario's" You know the:
What if I don't make it...?
What if it doesn't work...?
What if I hate it...?
What if something goes wrong for me...?
Who can I blame for this? It must be somebody's fault!

These people also focus on what they don't want. This is often the case for people losing weight. If you are continually focusing on not eating, not putting on weight, not having that roll/chocolate bar, you are doomed for failure. If however you ask yourself the questions in the exercise and turn your thoughts into positive affirmations, it is an excellent call for mindset change and brings you into E-Thinking.

E-Thinking lives in the desired place – just like your exercise above. E-Thinking focuses on what you will feel like when you get to your destination. E-Thinking doesn't focus on the "how to" and/or the nature of the task. E-thinking focuses on the end result.

E-Thinking provides aim and direction and brings prosperity to your personal and business life!

Six Principles of E-Thinking

1. Focus on what you want, not what you don't want and BELIEVE you can achieve
2. Know what the Result will look like and know that you DESERVE it
3. Know that you have not yet achieved your full potential
4. Have markers in place to work to – so you know if you are on course
5. Work out what resources you need
6. Have a Timed Action Plan and stick to it like glue!

"Desire is the key to motivation, but it's the determination and commitment to an unrelenting pursuit of your goal - a commitment to excellence - that will enable you to attain the success you seek"

Mario Andretti

Thinking BIGG

This is my favourite starter before any goal setting takes place. The way I see it, goals have to fit the SMART model which I'll tell you more about later.

Before we get onto practical goal setting, let's have a bit of fun!

You have already thought about what you would you do if you knew you couldn't fail; now I want you to think what huge goals you could have in your mind for the future – in this exercise I don't want you to consider any practicalities. Let your imagination go wild on this one!

I have talked a lot about the qualities of successful people and the clear way that it is the big picture or the end result that they think of. Whether you like Richard Branson or not, put yourself on Necker Island for a moment, position yourself in the hammock overlooking the sea and think big.

When I say think big – I mean think of BIGG Goals. These are:

Bullish &
Incredible &
Great
Goals

These goals aren't usually exact, they don't meet the SMART profile of goal setting (specific, measurable, achievable, realistic and timed) but they are your dreams and your dreams should have no boundaries.

There are SIX rules you to follow when creating your BIGG's

BIGG's need to be:

1. Short and to the point
2. Goals you feel strongly about that fit in with your emotions, desires and values
3. Ideas that you may think are impossible (for now...)
4. They are not things you are about to start working on now (they would be goals, not BIGG's)
5. Creative
6. Long Term – 5-25 years

Examples of BIGG's can include:
1. To write a book and become a published author
2. To start an airline (one of mine!)
3. To become a millionaire
4. To start a business

So have a go by writing down your THREE BIGG's. Keep a note of them in your wallet, on your fridge or keep this book safe with them written in and dated. You will be surprised how E-Thinking and Thinking BIGG can help these goals fall write into your lap as if like magic.

When you write down your three, try and put together anything such as an image, book, company profile – anything which brings your BIGG's to life! Keep them in clear view and use them to inspire you!

BIGG ONE

BIGG TWO

BIGG THREE

Goal Setting for Success

Rather than try and sell the benefits of Goal Setting. I thought this may be best to start with the Yale Study that I picked up whilst at University and starting my goal setting off.

This is how I remember it...

Yale Study

In 1953 Yale University conducted a study of their graduating students. Goal Setting is a large part of teaching at Yale and the University was surprised to discover that only 3% of the Class of 53 had set themselves goals for success and emotionally committed to them.

They key measurement for students is Exam Results and Grades.

Yale tracked this 3% and discovered that the 3% of students who had set themselves goals had outperformed the other 97% by achieving higher grades and these results were overwhelming!

These students continued to use Goal Setting as a way of life. In 1973 Yale carried out yet another study on Class of 53, the results were again astounding. In the only 2 areas they could measure, financial achievement & Career success, the 3% had outperformed the other 97% with phenomenal differences!

It is widely accepted that Goal Setting is an aid to success in life and careers – particularly since the days of 1953. However people still seem to either shy away from setting goals or don't reach their goals and I have thought about the reasons why...

"People are not lazy. They simply have impotent goals – that is goals that do not inspire them"

Tony Robbins

So why don't people set goals when it's widely accepted that GOAL SETTING is a real tool to aid success?

I'd say there were four main reasons for this:

1. People like to continue to follow their norm and I think John Henry Fabre's well known story of the processional caterpillars proves this point. The fact is clear. You cannot continue doing something over and over again and expecting that one day you will get a different result.
2. People believe that they are not worthy. "Why should something good ever happen to me?" They believe that good things only happen to other people. This is simply not true.
3. FEAR – it's the line of least resistance and the biggest enemy to success. It's imperative to press on regardless. I think Susan Jeffers titled her book pretty well with – "Feel the fear and do it anyway!"
4. People don't know how...they literally have never been alert to the idea of goal setting and/or just don't know how to go about it.

Once you know the formula to setting goals, you can apply it to any area in your grid of life. However, before I continue I have some good news and bad news. As always, let me start with the bad..

The bad news is that real goal setting takes between 10 and 20 hours, some times 30 for more complex goals.

The good news is that the focus and direction that this initial investment gives you, will mean that you have an extra 3 hours a day to play with.

Goal setting is like everything else in life:
First you do the work then you reap the benefits.

There are many things that will stop you setting goals or attaining them. It's usually the voice in your head and I often here the same old stories – do any of these sound familiar?

People say things like:

- I'm not ready just yet
- I don't have time at the moment
- I need a partner to help me
- I need to put all my plans together before I start!
- Oh I need more money to start that
- I'm waiting until we have better weather
- I'm waiting until we get our new brochures

Or worse:
- I'm going to start on Monday
- I'm going to start next week
- I'm starting next January!

More like – I'm never ever going to start. These are the worst pitfalls – the "I'm gonna do-ers" More like, "The never do-ers!"

So what can you do to avoid this? Here are four easy tips!

- ✓ Emotionally commit yourself
- ✓ Utilise pictures to visualise yourself at your goal
- ✓ Know where you are going
- ✓ Make better use of your time!

Napoleon was once said to have claimed, he won so many battles because he understood the value on 5 minutes.

"Vision without action is merely a dream. Action without vision just passes the time. Vision with action can change the world."

Joel A. Barker

Goal Setting in Six Easy Steps (Following the SMART Methodology)

1)   Identify what you want to achieve and imagine what achieving this goal would mean to you, what else will you get if you have this? Write down your SPECIFIC goal, make sure you are clear about what you want. Make sure you understand how this goal can be MEASURED and make sure this is a MEASURABLE goal so you know if you are on your route and when you have got there.

2)   Emotionally commit to your goal – write it down and think – If you have this, what higher purpose does this fulfil? Is this goal at least 25% ACHIEVABLE? Is it possible and is it REALISTIC? What sort of person will this make you? Make sure this goal is a MUST for you.

3)   Identify the obstacles that stand in your way – what is stopping you from getting this? How are you going to overcome them?

4)   Select your "A" Team (more on this in Chapter 3) Seek out the people/groups/organisations that can help you reach your goal

5)   Work out what you need to know and prepare a plan of action with a deadline of when you need to achieve your goal. This goal must be TIMED and must have a deadline for attainment.

6)   Take MASSIVE ACTION TODAY to start work on achieving your goal.

Now consider this...if you had this right now, would you take it?

Exercise - My goals

Ok so let's have a go. I am an avid goal setter and I have plucked from my goal sheets my three year plan to write this book which I thought may provide an example or guideline for you to follow. I wrote the actual goal with a TIMED element of 3 years but worked backwards so the goal was measurable each step of the way. I hope it helps...

Here is an example plan which is based on the following goal: 'to write a successful book that is accepted by a publisher with global reach, which sells over 100,000 copies within 3 years.'

3 years
Publish an updated edition. Sell 200,000 copies worldwide. Have a draft of the first chapter of my next book.

2 years
Sell over 25,000 copies in the UK. Have the book translated into at least two other languages and have sold 10,000 out of the UK. Gain 10 interviews overseas

18 months
Launch book and gain six interviews with newspapers, magazines or radio

Within 12 months
Finish drafts of all six chapters ready for proof reading and editing

Within 6 months
Finish drafts of four chapters and decide on publishing

Within 3 months
Research the market and current products. Get together an "A Team" to help with all areas I need assistance with, get writing the second chapter

Within 1 month
Get a title and an idea of the 6 chapters and start putting together to first chapter

Within 1 week
Decide 10 ideas I want to research and put into the book, start writing

Now have a go at working backwards with your goals. Make sure they fit the "Goal Setting in Six Easy Steps" Methodology.

YOUR GOALS:

Within 3 years

Within 2 years

Within 18 months

Within 12 months

Within 6 months

Within 3 months

Within 1 Month

Within 1 Week

Before you move on, can you push yourself any harder?   Take another look at your goals...

"There is an interesting world out there, not always pretty, but none the less certainly the basic material to be so.

We need more men & women of great vision, who can stand back and look at an area of great bareness and isolation, recognising the potential of just what it could be.

No matter what your start in life, by way of status or intellect, nothing is more important than embarking on that great voyage of discovery and change.

But you must first embark to commence any voyage, is wise to check all the best maps and charts, tried and proven, check the weather forecasts and once well prepared, pay the fare corresponding to how and where you wish to go in life.

Life as I see it is like a Sea voyage, we cannot hope to see some of the most interesting places without leaving the safety of the harbour"

ANON

The SAP Success Model

My research brought a formula for success which I call the SAP success model.

Successful Imagery

Action

Persistence

This three step process is what I feel is THE way to get yourself on the road to success. Have a go!

Successful Imagery

Step One is to imagine yourself successful.

Form a picture in your mind about what you will look like, how you will feel, what job you will be doing (if any!), what house you will live in, what family and friends will be around you?

Now put this into words and create a scrapbook of all the images you see in newspapers and magazines that coincide with your successful self.

The imagination is a powerful force.

These images will be a vision of your reality through effort and goal setting. Always keep these in mind.

What's holding you back? People usually only picture or think about the negatives and do not focus on the positives. If you think you will fail, you will. Conversely if you think you can be successful, you can.

So now let's put this together.

This involves you picturing how you see yourself being successful, your picture of success. With this picture in mind note the intricate details and write them down. Outline what you need to do to make this picture a reality.

Action

Many people have good ideas and talk about what they want to do or who they want to be but never put those thoughts into action.

People are held back by many things, mostly lack of support, lack of self-belief and the possibility of failure. You can have a good idea or even a great one, but it only becomes successful once it is brought to action.

It takes 24 hours for a good idea to fade.

If no action is taken within 24 hours, was it that great an idea? Even if you take a small step of action, you know you have started and it is worth pursuing.

Taking one step and then another is what keeps the enthusiasm alive and the drive towards success.

Persistence

Continue once you have made your initial steps and maintain your action through your idea.

The people who become truly successful have this to thank – PERSISTENCE. You can only move forward if you work tirelessly and continue on your journey of success.

Nothing will stand in your way and if something comes along, then why not figure out a way to knock it down or move past it.

Nothing is impossible but only you have the power to drive your success.

The SAP Success Model is now yours to put into action.

First get yourself in the right frame of mind and the only way to do this is to work on yourself through NLP techniques. I am sure some of you have heard of it, studied it or are even practitioners but I am about to unveil it in my own way. I hope this helps.

"To be successful, the first thing to do is fall in love with your work"

Sister Mary Lauretta

Mind Control through NLP

Whether you are an expert or a beginner or have even never heard of NLP, I feel this is a brief and worthwhile introduction or reaffirmation of what is an excellent way to program your mind for success.

Getting in the right frame of mind is imperative to achieve success. So why did I choose NLP?

NLP studies brilliance and is the method for studying brilliance
NLP studies excellence and is the method for studying excellence

In the 70's a linguist, John Grinder and a mathematician, Richard Brandler, studied people who were excellent communicators and who had the ability for personal change. These people included world class therapists, business leaders and people at the top of their game in fields such as Sales. This study produced findings which provide a "How to" approach – that is "how to be who you want to be" "how to get what you want" and how to react and behave differently than your automatic response i.e. how to react differently to events. Grinder and Brandler believed that the tools and techniques derived from NLP provides the ability to "copy" from the experts to ensure success.

NLP stands for Neuro-Linguistic Programming. Neuro refers to the nervous system, the mental paths to our five senses. Linguistic refers to our non-verbal language such as gestures, posture and habits that reveals our thinking styles. Programming is used as it insinuates that our thoughts, feelings and actions can be altered or changed completely. To recap:

N – Neurology   The mind and how we **think**
L – Linguistics   What we **say**, verbally and non-verbally
P – Programming   What we **do** to achieve our goals

So it's clear that NLP refers to the study of excellence and is the ability to be ones best more frequently. NLP is an influential and realistic method for self development and change.

My interpretation of the Principles of NLP or the Pillars of NLP as they are sometimes called are as follows:

Principles of NLP

1. You are the first principle of NLP. You and your emotional status along with your skill level are the most important part of NLP. Only you can make NLP happen in your behaviour. NLP is used by an individual but can be used well or badly. Your success depends on your resourcefulness and your ability to "walk your talk and talk your walk"

2. The presuppositions of NLP explained below are those guiding principles that are taken for granted which influence your success of NLP.

3. Rapport is the ability to form lasting, quality relationships with mutual trust and respect. You develop a good rapport through understanding others and respecting their beliefs and thoughts and is achieved through good communication. I see it as "mirroring' because if you can speak the language of the person you are speaking to and mirror their actions, your communication will improve immensely.

4. The outcome is a vital principle of NLP. You need to know what it is you want to achieve as well as understanding the outcomes of others. NLP is best achieved through outcome based thinking and is done by firstly knowing what your current situation is, what your desired outcome is and then the strategy to wards achieving it.

5. Feedback is extremely influential in achieving successful NLP as you need to know if you are moving towards the desired outcome and you will only know this through feedback. Are you getting feedback and are you listening to it? Your

feedback needs to be accurate in order for you to know if you are proceeding as you planned and moving towards your outcomes.

6. You need to be flexible and adaptable. If what you are doing is not working then you need to alter your behaviour and act differently for different results. I love the well coined phrase "insanity is doing the same thing over and over again and expecting different results".

Also learn the presuppositions and you will be well on your way to mind control and success through NLP:

Presuppositions of NLP

1. People learn from their own experiences and use these experiences to form their understanding of reality. Reality is not reality to an individual unless it has been experienced. However people respond to their experience and not to reality itself. It is the response to an event which creates the outcome, not the event itself.

2. We have the ability to do anything. Nothing is impossible. If someone can or has done something, you can learn and you can achieve it too and modelling successful performance leads to excellence!

3. We are always communicating – we are unable to not communicate. Even if you were trying not to communicate, you would be communicating that you are uninterested, bored, silent etc. Remember that communication is not what you intend to say, rather what someone "hears"

4. The mind and the body form part of a system. They function interdependently of each other. If one is altered then that will have an affect on the other and in turn alter that. For example, when we think differently, our bodies change and when we act differently, we feel differently.

5. All actions and behaviour whatever the outcome has positive intentions. Every action provides a positive intention – it is always meant for a reason with an outcome. For example, if you reprimand someone, the intention is positive, to alter their bad behaviour.

6. People make the best choices at that time with the knowledge, experiences and resources they have available to them at that specific point in time. With time and different experiences, different decisions can be made but at the time of a decision, it is made best to that person's knowledge.

7. If you continue to do the same things you will continue to gain the same outcomes. Do something new to achieve something new. In order to understand and gain new perspectives or new knowledge and insights, you need to act and have the experience.

How are you going to learn the skills and techniques you need to control or unleash the power of the mind through NLP? Well first let's examine the Learning Matrix.

Learning is a natural phenomenon and involves personal development. We learn to act differently, think differently and feel differently. Learning takes place constantly and most of the time unconsciously, adapting to changing situations and changing environments.

The Learning Matrix is divided into four stages and I am going to take the example of learning to drive to explain the levels of learning:

1. Unconscious incompetence. At one time in your life you weren't even aware of it and didn't know how to do it.
2. Conscious incompetence. You've just started to learn to drive but you aren't very good. You learn fast at this stage, but because the less you know, the more the room for improvement. Your results are immediate.
3. Conscious competence. You have passed your test and you feel fairly confident that you know hot to drive. The you have to go onto a busy motorway to improve your level but improvement is more difficult to achieve. The better you are at something, the more the effort is needed to make a noticeable change.
4. Unconscious competence. You have been driving for say 6 years and now you don't have to think about it. You find yourself on the M42 not knowing when you joined the motorway from the M40. You can do it without even thinking about it! This is where you want to get to with the techniques of NLP. If you can behave and perform and act differently in the unconscious competence state, this leaves your mind free to concentrate on other things.

To learn any new skill you can preserve yourself of use a coach to increase motivation and segment your learning into bite size goals. Or you can use NLP as a form of accelerated learning where you can jump from stage one to stage four on the learning matrix.

So how do you use NLP for Mind Control?

Have a go at two exercises that will help you apply the teaching of NLP:

Exercise One – NLP in Action

Situation – You have a sales presentation with a difficult client tomorrow and you feel like you will never get the business as the odds are stacked against you...

Exercise – Imagine you are in the meeting room and the client has shaken your hand and said they would be delighted to grant you the contract. How do you feel, what does the room look like? When are you going to call your boss, imagine what they will say...Imagine going home to your partner and telling them you got the deal.

How great do you feel?

Now do this exercise before you go into that meeting and remember the principles and presuppositions of NLP. Remember your client wants you to get this deal, remember to: mirror their communication style, remember what outcome you want, focus on your presentation, have a positive intention and purpose, see yourself winning!

Exercise Two – NLP in Action

Situation – You never get round to doing something e.g. writing that book!

Exercise – Imagine yourself at the book launch, how your mother and father are bursting with pride, how great you feel at your accomplishment, how all it took was to start writing...

How great do you feel?

Now imagine that "book" or whatever it is. Close you eyes and think where is it – is it to the side of you, behind you? Now grab it and move it right in front of you, full yourself with energy, start to feel a rise in motivation, start to remember yourself in the room when you have accomplished it! Now open your eyes and START IT!

It's easy isn't it? If you put this mind control into all the exercise we have discussed such as Goal Setting, you will see greater results!

"Most successful men have not achieved their distinction by having some new talent or opportunity presented to them. They have developed the opportunity that was at hand"

Bruce Barton

Blood, Sweat and Careers

......Six Steps to Exceptional Career
Performance

Step 3

– Gather Your "A" Team

"You have to do it by yourself but
...you cannot do it alone!"
Martin Rutte

Gather Your "A" Team

Successful people always have a team around them and a key aspect of E-Thinkers is the ability to surround themselves with the right people. An "A" Team is like having your own board of directors who will help you gain real progress in your business and personal life, share your endeavours, provide a support system for you and provide you with experience, skill, talent and confidence!

Each and every day I associate with people who are either experts in the fields I am interested in, inspiring and supportive or brimming with energy and enthusiasm. There are potentially many people that you spend your time with now who can help you achieve exceptional career performance. It takes a good blend of people to work together to all achieve real benefit from forming a mastermind team, your "A" Team.

Like Rutte said – "You have to do it yourself but you cannot do it alone" so imagine for a minute you had say 6 people whom you met with regularly and whose focus was to fast track you to success, how would you feel? What impact would this have on your goals?

Who are the ten people you spend most of your time with?

Are at least 50% of them able to help you achieve phenomenal success?

I think you agree that you have to do things differently to get different results and changing your associations is a change for the better. Trust me; you will be amazed by what happens!

How do you choose your team?

Your aim is to surrounded by intelligent, enthusiastic people with specific skills who make you want to exceed your present reach. First let's start by who you know in your circles. Write down, any people who can teach/train/inspire/motivate/support you or move your career along either directly or indirectly with their knowledge or contacts.

Category	Who do I know who can teach/mentor/train/ inspire/motivate or support me?
Family	
Friends	
Friends of Friends or Acquaintances	
Colleagues and Ex Colleagues	
Customers and Ex Customers	
Suppliers and Ex Suppliers	
People I know in the industry I want to develop in?	

If you are struggling to get the right people, consider this...

What parties do you go to?

I have done lots of work in the Professional Services Marketing Sector and met executives at the number 2 position desperately trying to get their next promotion. One thing amazes me is how few parties they go to! When I say parties, I am afraid I am actually talking industry sector events...

We have two main membership bodies in this sector – the PSMG and the PM Forum – both excellent at providing training, conferences, free events and regular drinks. Now these seminars and drinks are always focused purely on the niche sector professionals. If you go along to an event and are speaking to someone, there is at least an 80% chance they will be working in a similar (+/-) position in a competitor firm. The 20% are usually recruiters or suppliers to the industry – still great people to meet!

These seminars are great for learning, profile raising and more importantly making contacts. Yet so few people who want to excel in their career actually maximise this opportunity.

So how do you go about getting yourself to the right parties?

Simple:
- ✓ Search on the internet for membership organisations attached to your sector
- ✓ Read your trade press and relevant membership websites
- ✓ Look on "linked in" for contacts in your area, see which groups they belong to and contact/view to see what events are being organised

Networking to Win

Networking is an essential tool for gathering your "A" Team and maximising your contacts. Career Professionals also claim that between 50-70% of people secure themselves a new role through their contact base.

So why aren't you doing it?

It seems the best way to accelerate your career...

Putting together your "A" Team will undoubtedly grow your network and encourage more wins for you. Not only will you gain valuable knowledge on the industry through your contact base, you will also have a "heads up" on what's happening in the market.

A Win Win Situation!

So what happens now?

Create a long list of people from your networks and current contacts and approach them, you ideally want 4-8 people, no more. Some of you may have people you know pretty well and some of you may keep it to purely professional contacts. Here's some examples on what to say to them...

"Hi Julie, I have just undertook a personal development plan and thought about getting a group together where we could share ideas/market knowledge and keep a track of our goals. It's called a Mastermind Group and I've handpicked some likeminded people to start it, would you be interested in joining?"

"I'm putting together a "think tank" for ambitious people in our industry who want to progress their career and I thought of you. We will get together once a month, share ideas and action plans and work on our objectives to move forward. I have one space left, would you be interested in taking it?"

I have my team, what now?

Ok, now you have your team in place, I have put together six steps to kick start your group and get it off the ground.

Six Steps to creating a Successful "A" Team!

1. Arrange a meeting date and time and suitable venue. Make sure it's appropriate e.g. quite (ish), with a table, chairs, pen, paper, drinks etc
2. Welcome the group and start by asking if you can all set out a mission statement and a list of objectives for the group.
3. Decide on frequency and times for subsequent meetings.
4. Create a template or give each member a piece of paper and ask that each person write out their name, contact details, background, network, achievements and what they expect to get out of this group.
5. Ask for each individual to write down the goals they wish to share with the rest of the group and what help they need in achieving those goals.
6. Ask each person to write down what they will commit to doing by the next meeting that will both get them closer to their goal and help one of the other members.

Tips for Success

✓ Photocopy all the contact sheets and goals to provide everyone with a comprehensive copy for their file
✓ Write an agenda for each meeting and keep notes and make sure everyone writes down their own action for the meeting
✓ Let everyone have equal chance to speak to talk over what they have done since the last meeting (including their action point) and what help they need
✓ Keep the meetings incredibly fun, short and to the point
✓ Make sure you raise the energy in the room and keep up the pace!

Remember that your "A" Team's objective is to raise the bar of your members by challenging each other to create and implement goals, brainstorm ideas, and support each other with total honesty, respect and compassion.

This concept was introduced by Napoleon Hill in the early 1900's. In his timeless classic, "Think And Grow Rich" he wrote about the Mastermind principle as:

"The coordination of knowledge and effort of two or more people, who work toward a definite purpose, in the spirit of harmony."

Napoleon Hill

Blood, Sweat and Careers

......**Six Steps** to Exceptional Career
Performance

Step

– Dig for Opportunities

Dig for Opportunities

How do you go about getting the job you want? How do you keep up to date with the opportunities within your chosen field? How do you ensure you are maximising your success?

Well one thing is for sure, there are a variety of ways to look for opportunities in the market – all of which have advantages and disadvantages. No one method is better than another and all are required to ensure you have a strong stake in your market place.

Some of the techniques you will have experienced are as follows:

Traditional Methods of Securing Opportunities
- ✓ Newspaper Advertising
- ✓ Magazines and Trade Press
- ✓ Word of Mouth
- ✓ Recruiters – local, national, international
- ✓ Headhunters
- ✓ Speculative Applications

Modern Methods of Securing Opportunities
- ✓ Powerful Networking and Referrals
- ✓ Company Websites
- ✓ The Internet Job Boards
- ✓ Posting your CV on the Internet and waiting
- ✓ Signing up for Email Alerts
- ✓ Job Sites such as:

- www.monster.co.uk (All)
- www.totaljobs.com (All)
- www.cwjobs.com (IT)
- www.reed.co.uk (Trainee and General)
- www.jobs.guardian.co.uk (Media/Marketing)
- www.thelawyer.com/jobs (Law)
- www.google.co.uk can be used to search any specialised job by typing in the job title you are searching for

Job Search Techniques – Fact v Fiction

Responding to job advertisements is an interesting game and in my opinion a low value way of securing a position. With the market the way it is you are almost entering a lottery each time you apply as the response levels go up and up. The other problem is that employers or recruiters seem to achieve a 10% success rate of matches from job advertisements which means they have to plough through 90% of people who aren't suitable to find you!

There are two types of job seekers:

The **Reactive** Job Seeker reacts to opportunities they see without much application. Perhaps through job adverts or they get a call about an opportunity through a friend or they leave their CV on monster and wait for an agency call. Think about how you or your partner got your last job. Through friends, ex colleagues, word of mouth, a recruiter or head hunter?

The **Proactive** Job Seeker prepares a Plan of Attack, identifies their opportunities and target clients and goes and gets the job they actually want...not just what's lying around on the market.

As I said before, between 50-70% of jobs get filled before formally coming out to market. Therefore to advance your career you need to make some smart moves.

I'm not going to bore you with how to apply for jobs...but I am going to focus on three sure fire ways to dig out opportunities:

1. How to unearth The Hidden Opportunities on the Net
2. How to work with Recruiters successfully
3. How to make Speculative Applications

These are the secret tools for career advancement!

The Hidden Opportunities on the Net

There is no doubt that online networking is a major source of contacts and a great way to secure a new role.

Do you have "Twitterific" on your "iphone" to be following the right people to take your career forward? Are you using "myspace" and "facebook" as a business networking site rather than to liaise with friends?

If not, why not?

Do you know what these sites can do for you?

Twitter aside, there are lots of different sites out there and ones in my opinion that are perhaps more business/career focused such as ZoomInfo and Career Builder. However, the word on the street is that LinkedIn is used by nearly a fifth of the UK's white collar population! Are you one of these? Whatever the answer, I want you to make sure you are using this to its highest potential.

My favourites for securing networks, contacts and opportunities are LinkedIn, Facebook and Xing, so let's have a look at them in depth.

LinkedIn – Free Membership for a Basic Account

This is probably the most career focused of all the social networking sites. It describes itself as an online network of more than 42 million users from around the world! The company has said that it is growing by 1m users every 17 days!

LinkedIn claims that through your network you can find potential clients, service providers, subject experts, partners, business opportunities, jobs and likeminded professionals. In my opinion, this is a great way to expand your contacts. You can easily search for individuals from a particular firm or with a particular job title. As you can search by company go and find people who work in your target firm and contact them. An upgrade to your membership is usually a shrewd investment if you discover an array of contacts.

You can also become members of groups such as trade bodies, company groups etc. Then you get regular feedback telling you what's going on in that sector/group or company.

The key is to have as many contacts as you can and as many recommendations. Get registered now and ask people to recommend you and connect with you, you will quickly see your numbers grow.

Facebook – Free Membership for a Basic Account

A well known site usually for social networking, however, do not dismiss this one so easily for job searching and networking. It has a great "group facility" so you can connect with people who work for one of your target firms through one of their groups. You can then read the discussion board, post messages and work towards your new opportunity with that firm.

There are lots of hidden opportunities and contacts on this site!

Xing – Free Membership for a Basic Account

Xing has been operating in Europe for a few years but only now beginning to make its mark in the UK. The site claims to have over 7 million users in over 200 countries! This is a particularly good site for opportunities in Europe. It has excellent groups that you can join targeted to your specific interest or company. You will need premium membership to Xing to contact people who are not currently your contacts.

Other sites to investigate: Career Builder, myspace, Twitter

Working with Recruiters

Unfortunately recruiters have a bad name. When the truth is they do one of the most important jobs for businesses by securing them the best talent in the market! They also find people brand new positions and gainful employment when they are out of work. Yet this part of what they do often gets swept under the table.

Whether or not you consider recruiters to be a necessary evil, they are necessary, they are real people doing a tough job and here is how to get the best from them.

Ten Ways to get the best out of recruiters!

1. Always talk to the right people – those in the industry you work in that understand your background. Never register with generalist agencies – this is a waste of time.
2. Prepare a longlist of SIX recruiters in your niche area – check out what jobs they are advertising on their website to see how active they are. Talk to your friends in the sector for referrals and then talk to the six recruiters.
3. Choose 3 who you like the sound of, who have the experience you require and who want to meet you within the week. Only submit your CV to these Top 3.
4. Meet with your consultant at each of these agencies. If one makes an excellent pitch to remain with them exclusively for two weeks and you feel they will look after you and have enough opportunities and market presence, take the offer! It could really work in your favour.
5. Make sure your agency provides you with a Workseekers Agreement – expected in law and so often not provided by cowboy outfits.
6. At your meeting, have a list of questions prepared. Make sure you prepare for this meeting as if it is an interview...be smart, well prepared and positive. The recruiter is a person after all and will work harder for people who make an effort and are a pleasure to deal with!

7. Make sure you prepare an Action Plan and a Contact Arrangement so you know when to call and what is happening.
8. Keep in regular contact and return any messages left for you. If you don't they will assume you have found a role and won't be submitting you to their new role that they were calling you about.
9. Ask (and take) advice from your recruiter – on your interview style and CV.
10. If you like what you see, refer a friend, this will ensure your recruiter works extra hard to return the favour to you!

Ten questions to ask your recruiter:

1. How you performed at interview
2. What version of your CV they will be submitting
3. If they have any reservations about finding you a role
4. What the market is like
5. What opportunities they have and are anticipating coming up with their clients
6. What you need to do to succeed
7. Which of their team members work on the same kind of positions and if you can meet them
8. What other training and experience you ought to get to advance to the next step
9. What their opinion is of the salary and package you are expecting
10. What you can do to make sure they submit you to all their opportunities

A good recruiter will never send your CV to a prospective employer without first asking your permission and providing a company background. Ensure you are always told:

- The company history, direction, strategy and structure
- The job title, responsibilities, salary, team structure, manager profile

Prepare your Recruiter Longlist

Recruiter	Agency	Tel No	Notes	Interview date/form

Keep track of the opportunities presented to you:

Recruiter	Company/ position	Role	Salary	Interview 1	Interview 2

Making Speculative Applications

This is such an underused tool and a great way for you to achieve the role you want whether it's advertised or not! Firstly, you need to do your research. Research the industry you want to work in and the company/companies as below:

Industry Research – find out:
- What are the regulatory bodies in charge of this industry?
- Is there an industry association or professional body that could aid your research?
- What is the size of the industry?
- Is it stable/in decline/in growth?
- Is it international/national/european?
- How is it formed (small/big/multi clients)?
- Who are the major players (key companies) in this industry?
- Who are the companies you want to work for?
- How are they performing?
- Who are their competitors and how are they performing?
- Is this a viable industry?
- What's the key news in the industry?

Company Research – find out:
- Background Information – what is the size of the company, type (PLC/LTD), market share, financial data including turnover/profit?
- What is the nature of the business?
- Is it stable/in decline/in growth?
- Is it international/national/european?
- How many employees in all locations?
- What products and services does it offer?
- How are they performing?
- Who are their competitors and how are they performing?
- Is this a viable company?
- What's the key news in the company?
- Who are the key contacts you can network with?

Ok now you have done your research and are happy to go for the companies you have identified. Start today with my SIX Step Plan:

1. Find all relevant contacts via their website, LinkedIn and other internet sites and check if they do happen to be recruiting (irrelevant but its good for you to know)
2. Initiate Contact via email or letter – make sure your pitch is targeted to the right person, the one who will make the decision to hire. Don't send your CV at this stage!
3. Attract Attention via a "Hook" - for this use some of their news, reports, mergers or acquisition to show your interest. Alternatively use the hook about the person you are writing to – from your internet research
4. Gain Interest – Sell yourself and tell them about your achievements and how it will add (preferably to the bottom line!) to their firm
5. Close with Impact! – Tell them you will be contacting them in the next seven days to check safe receipt and see how you could benefit the firm
6. Follow up! And get a meeting, ask for an exploratory one so you can tell them what is happening and your current firm and some of the projects you have been working on…

Here's how to make that call!

"Hello. My name is Angela Cahill. I have heard about the great work you are doing at X firm and actually dropped you a note just last week. I'm actually looking for a move and although I am active in my job hunt, I didn't want to do anything before having the opportunity of meeting you. My main skills are…..and I feel this could benefit your firm in this way…. would you be kind enough to spare 15 minutes to hear more about your firm and so I can be best placed to apply for a position as it comes up? I'd be happy to meet at a time and place convenient to you?"

Now you need some tools! A Winning CV and Letter of Application won't just provide you with some open doors, it's also chance for you to cement in your mind what makes you so special!

Ten things to do today to get the job you want!

1. Send a handwritten note.
2. Clip and send an article of interest.
3. Talk to a satisfied client you have worked with and ask if they think their firm could be interested in you
4. Send a thank-you card to someone who referred you.
5. Give your business card to someone with influence.
6. Send a letter to the editor of a magazine your potential employer reads.
7. Add fifteen people to your mailing list and email them.
8. Leave a compelling voice mail.
9. Make an appointment.
10. Call a client you haven't talked to in two years.

Blood, Sweat and Careers

......**Six Steps** to Exceptional Career
Performance

Step 5

– Create A Winning Pitch

Creating A Winning Pitch

How much time do you put into preparing your CV and letter of application for each position you go for?

If it's less than an hour, it's not enough and that's only if your CV is a perfect document to start with!

To a prospective employer, you are a piece of paper. So that piece of paper needs to be good, wouldn't you say? I'd say it needs to be phenomenal. It is essential that you create the right tools in order to succeed. This whole process is a game of strategy and tactics and those that play it well, get the opportunities they deserve.

Writing a Phenomenal CV

This document can be called Curriculum Vitae, Resume and Profile etc. There is no universally accepted format for instance in europe it is common to have a photograph of yourself on your CV. This is neither common practice nor advised in the UK!

But wherever you live or want to work a CV must clearly explain to the reader what it is you can do for them and should never be a list of your work places or skills.

A CV should be:
1. A well presented, **sales** document. This makes all the difference!
2. A source of interesting and relevant information and shows what achievements you have that will benefit your next employer.
3. It forms the basis of your interview and is the focus of your conversation with a potential employer

A CV is not to get you a job *rather to get you an interview* and *act as a reminder* to the interviewer of who you are and what you are about.

Some Key Hints on Preparation:

- **Make it easy on the eye**! Lots of white space to make it easy to read, they are usually read on screen!
- **Avoid unusual fonts or graphics**. Most CVs are circulated electronically and not all fonts can be read on all PC's..
- **Don't leave drawing up or updating your CV to the last minute!** So many people send whatever they have on file. If you really want to create impact and get the job you are applying for, take your time.
- **Don't consider your CV to be finished......**it is a working document that must be amended for any position you apply for.
- **Make it an interesting read**......cut out any waffle, stick to the point. Use inspirational language, sell yourself!
- **Use sensible headings......**Personal Details, Career to date, Education.
- **Make sure it is no more than 2 pages long**
- **Use a Standard Format including:**

    1. Personal details – name, address, telephone numbers, email and date of birth
    2. Profile – 3/4 sentences that summaries you and want you can bring the organisation
    3. Education and Qualifications
    4. Career to Date: latest role/job first, be sure to include the length of time you have been working there, your title, your responsibilities and what you achieved while there.
    5. Additional information e.g. non work related achievements.
    6. Hobbies and Interests – keep them team orientated sports and similar.
    7. Skills/IT Skills

There are different styles of CVs. Choose a style that is relevant to your career history and the job you are applying for.

You can choose different formats for your CV depending on your career objective and personal taste. Here is an overview of the main formats.

Responsibilities: These CVs are usually written in job description style, emphasising title and responsibilities. Some people actually use their job description to cut and paste onto their CV. These CVs indicate nothing about achievement and tell the reader what you were supposed to do, not what you do.

Chronological: These CVs start with a summary of your experience and your key skills. This is followed by your work history, most recent positions first. Achievements are usually placed in each section.

Functional: Here, CVs start with your relevant achievements, followed by your work experience. These are useful to give a wow factor when you are changing careers and want to talk about your transferable skills as you work history may not be relevant.

Skills Based: These CVs are useful when you are applying for jobs which require knowledge of specific technologies and are useful in the IT or Technical Industries.

Industry specific: CVs – some industries for example PR and Law want their applications to outline their key new stories or cases/deals. These work for only a handful of industries

My opinion is to always go for either a Chronological or Functional CV. I actually prefer the Chronological approach with detailed achievements both in the body of the email and within the profile.

Before you put together your winning CV, I need you to dig down into your achievements. These are your key hooks and form your offering to an employer.

I'd like you to think of five and consider for each one –

1. The impact this had on the company or market or industry and/or
2. The impact this had on the bottom line (sales/profit) and/or
3. How this increased productitvity and/or
4. How this increased the company image in a measurable way and/or
5. The impact on the department/people

Achievement 1

What was the situation?

What action did you take?

What was the outcome?

What was the effect?

The way I felt afterwards

Achievement 2

What was the situation?

What action did you take?

What was the outcome?

What was the effect?

Achievement 3

What was the situation?

What action did you take?

What was the outcome?

What was the effect?

Achievement 4

What was the situation?

What action did you take?

What was the outcome?

What was the effect?

Achievement 5

What was the situation?

What action did you take?

What was the outcome?

What was the effect?

Now prepare your CV. Here's an example layout:

Jeremy Burton-Jones

14 Goodhope Avenue
London
W1D 9FG
Mobile: 07966240004   Email: jbjones@freemail.com

Profile:

Successful, high calibre business development and relationship management professional with extensive experience working within both large corporate and professional services organisations and an established track record in business expansion with key achievements including:

- Best all round support staff performer in 2008 generating an additional £8million in revenue from new and existing clients
- Achieved 112% of target for lead generating activities
- Personally managed portfolio of 12 corporate clients ranging from £50M - £200M in turnover

Employment History

SQQ Accounting   **Jan 2007– Present**
Senior Business Development Manager

Responsibilities:
- Management of key clients and targets with the aim of developing new approaches, stream trends and niche services
- Management of the firms targeting 'Corporate 500' list
- Building relationships with key referrers (banks and solicitors) to encourage the referral of clients
- Line management of three junior BD executives
- Developed/coordinate marketing material and tender database for firms key regions

Key Achievements:
- Introduction of three "platinum" clients to the firm generating in excess of £3million in revenue
- Developed and implemented a new bid process resulting in a 37% increase in the firms win rate for new business.

Edenburgh LLP   **Feb 2003 – Dec 2006**
Client Development Manager

Responsibilities:
- Design and implementation of a sales process for the firms three key sectors
- Produce figures and trends in the corporate market aimed at the suitability of the service to ensure effective client targeting
- Research of competitor information and strategic market place activity to ensure new business opportunities were not overlooked

- 103 -

- Involvement in official tendering, pipeline reporting process, conference sales and support.

Key Achievements:
- Management of the "target client programme" resulting in the generation of over £2million in revenue
- Generated over 80 meetings with FTSE clients leading to 27 new introductions, resulting in new revenue generation.

SSC Accounting   **Dec 1998 – Jan 2002**

Regional Development Manager   **Feb 2000 – Jan 2002**
Regional Development Executive   Dec 1998 – Jan 2000

Responsibilities:
- Assist in identifying new prospects
- Act as the regional point of contact for clients
- Individually achieved £590K in revenue generation
- Maintain a comprehensive knowledge of core business services and encouraged cross selling between key sectors and services

Key Achievements:
- Project management of proposal bid, significantly contributing to the firms' biggest contract win worth over £15million.
- Achieved Top 5 national business developer in terms of financial results generating over £1,000,000 in new sales based upon 3-year figures

Education

Current   **CASS Business School, London**
              Masters in Business Administration

1995 - 1998   **University of Cambridge**
              Bachelor of Arts (Marketing) – 1st class Honours

1994   **St James' Grammer School**
              A levels: History (A) Theology (A) English Literature (B) Mathematics (A)
              GCSE's: English language (A) Science (B) Maths (A) Geography (A) History (A) Art (B) Design (B) English Literature (A) French (A) German (B)

A Winning Letter of Application!

Remember that your letter and your CV are the only things they know about you. They have to be good!

The Look

- Always typed and on A4 paper and produce a new letter for each application. Even if you have a template that you base your letter on, make sure you rewrite it. That way your letters will be fresh and alive, it's easy to spot the difference!
- Use a basic font, we recommend Arial, Arial Narrow or Times New Roman. Something easily readable on screen
- Make sure you have your name and address, their name and address, the date and the salutation matching the sign off e.g. if you address it to "Dear Sir/Madam" you end with "Yours faithfully", if you address it to say "Mr Taylor" you end with "Yours sincerely"

The Preparation

- Read the job advert, job description and requirements and tailor both your CV and application letter to suit that **ROLE** i.e. bring out the most relative points to match the job you are applying for. Revise your CV to highlight all the achievements relevant to this application and include it with your letter.
- Do your research on the company website and have powerful reasons as to why you would like to work for them
- Know who you should be addressing your letter to
- Explain clearly why you are suitable for the role

The Letter

- The letter should have three paragraphs 1st stating what you are applying for, where you saw the advert 2nd stating why you feel you are right for the role 3rd paragraph states that you would be happy to discuss this further and **will contact them to check safe receipt of your CV.**
- Keep a **record** of it in your job file
- Make sure you have the **recipient's name and address right**. Give the complete job reference / number from the ad.
- State your ability to meet the needs of the job. Use bullet points if you desire to show a correlation between your experience and what they are seeking.
- Focus on the advantage to them of employing you, not the advantage to you.
- The letter should be a maximum of one page long.

Here's an example...

EXAMPLE LETTER OF APPLICATION

Mr John Gilbert
43A Ravens Road
London
N21 1QQ

Mrs Puncher
Marketing Manger
CK Enterprises
130 Great West Road
Hammersmith
London
W6 9BA

17 July 2009

Dear Mrs Puncher

Re: Business Development Manager Position

I would like to apply for the above position (your reference MO/AC1), as advertised on the Monster website on the 16 July 2009. Please find attached a copy of my CV for your perusal.

I am currently working for CJ Enterprises in Business Development. I have 7 years experience within the sector, a degree in Marketing from Liverpool University and am currently hitting 180% of my sales target. You also requested a candidate who can speak two languages, I currently speak French and Spanish fluently and I am learning Japanese in my spare time. I have looked at the workings of your firm and your current acquisition of MJ Holdings and therefore feel this would be an excellent opportunity for me.

As I appreciate that you are likely to hear from a number of applicants for this position, I will contact you within the next two weeks to ensure that you have safely received my application. Thank you for taking the time to review my application.

Yours sincerely

John Gilbert
07850 005 006

Enc: CV

The Truth about Interviews

Being invited to interview is a major achievement. You would normally expect about one in ten of your job applications to lead to an interview especially if you are reacting to job advertisements. That is why it's essential to utilise recruiter relationships, speculative applications and the hidden opportunities on the net. This eliminates as much competition as possible and increases your interview rate by 75%!

The truth is:

They are not always positive
The interviewer is not always in the right frame of mind
They sometimes don't ask you the questions you would like!

Whenever you do go for an interview, use NLP Techniques to get you in the right frame of mind.

NLP Exercise – Interview Preparation

Sit down and close your eyes. Imagine you were the best person in your field, the greatest person on the market and you were brimming with confidence and happiness. Now imagine you are there in the interview room and everything is going well. The interviewers ask you about your strengths and skills and achievements and they are all at the forefront of your mind. They are desperate to hire you and as you are walking back to the tube station you get the call, offering you the role! How great does this feel?

I also believe in Mantra's to improve your confidence – try saying these three to yourself before your interviews!

My 3 Mantra's for Interview Success!

1. I know that my skills and achievements will greatly benefit this company!
2. I know I will do well and get offered this job!
3. I feel positive, I feel confident and I am in complete control!

Once you get to interview you are rarely more than two or three steps away from a job offer. So take your interviews seriously and prepare well.

Interview Questions

Here are some commonly asked interview questions which I'd strongly recommend you start to prepare answers for:

- What do you know about our firm/company?
- Why would you like to work for our company?
- Tell me about yourself...
- What are your 3 key strengths and what are your weaknesses?
- Why do you think you are suitable for this role/ for this type of organisation
- Tell me about a time you worked as part of a team?
- Talk me through your company and the issues it faces?
- Do you feel you have increased the company's profile?
- What does your typical day at work entail?
- What are/were your objectives/priorities in this role?
- Talk me through your work? Tell me about a piece of work you are proud of, from concept to completion?
- What do you feel is the biggest problem in your industry for at the moment?
- What are your key achievements in your current/last role?
- Talk me through the BD Strategy in your current/last role?
- What are your main objectives?
- How have you pro-actively increased the sector/ firm/specialism in the time you have been there? (Use your Revenue figures from starting the position to present date)
- What ways do you feel differentiate key clients from others and what is your strategy for Key Clients?
- How would you put together a target client list?
- How would you go about getting partners or fee earners on side?

So let's consider how you may answer one or two of these questions:

Question:

Tell me about yourself.

How to answer:

This is an ice breaker and often gives the interviewer a chance to settle down while learning a little about you. Please don't give your life story. Stick to what is relevant i.e. your work history that is relevant to the role for which you are applying. Be more detailed with present day information. Complete this by talking a little about your life outside work. Your answer should take no more than 1.5 - 2 minutes.

Question:

What do you see are the main objectives for this role?

How to answer:

Don't repeat the job description, just use the opportunity to sell back your relevant skills and experiences and how they fit the main objectives for the role.

Question:

Can you give me an example of a piece of work you are particularly proud of?

How to answer:

Make sure you always carry to an interview some examples of your work – perhaps a portfolio covering different projects you have worked on. Make sure you have rehearsed this one and have five or six bullet points on how to explain the piece of work and why it is particularly good and why you are particularly proud.

Question:

If you could turn back the clock, what would you have done differently in your career?

How to answer:

Always show you can make a mistake but learn from it, we all make mistakes. Make sure your answer isn't negative and isn't based on a recent example either.

Question:

Why are you leaving your current position?

How to answer:

If you are about to be made redundant or just have been, just be honest. If you hate your boss, your team, the culture – they just don't want to hear about it! Talk about the reasons why you would like to progress in your career and how this firm/opportunity provides that.

Competency Based Interview Questions

Most interviews contain some competency based questions these days. I've outlined some competencies, the questions that are asked and what the interviewer is looking for:

Competency	Question	Looking for
Customer Relationship	Who are the most difficult customers you have had to work with? What steps you take to ensure a productive, ongoing working relationship?	Empathy, patience, persistence, honesty. Good strategic approach to building relationships. Evidence of advanced people skills.
Coaching Mentoring	Can you describe a situation in which you actions have led directly to a real improvement in the work of a colleague? Have you taught new skills/methods to colleagues?	An encouraging, sensitive positive style. Good follow-on to ensure improvements are implemented. Evidence of interest in mentoring

Communication	When communicating complex technical issues to a non-technical audience, how do you ensure that you make yourself understood?	Proper qualification of level of understanding at the outset. Use of visual presentation aids, analogies. Able to keep things simple.
Influencing	Can you describe a situation in which you had to change the mind of a major customer in order to achieve the right results for that business?	Persistence. Presentation skills. Non-confrontational style. Example of success that has had a major impact on a business.
Flexibility	What is the most rapidly changing environment you have operated in? How did you deal with the particular demands of that situation?	Patience in dealing with constantly moving goal posts. Comfortable with ambiguity and change. Able to retain focus on key objectives.
Commercial Awareness	What is the most difficult negotiation you have had to enter into? Describe how you managed to achieve your objectives.	Good technical bargaining skills; making concessions, not revealing agenda etc. An ability to spot a good deal and then get it.

Accountability	Describe a completed piece of work that you are most proud of?	Takes ownership of work. Completes task properly. Taking real responsibility for end product.
Influencing & negotiating skills	Can you demonstrate an instance where you have been influential within your team and one of your ideas to improve a system for the benefit of the business has been taken on board?	Leadership Ability to persuade others to different point of view for good of business Diplomacy Success in negotiations
Logical approach	Can you think of an example where you have been faced with a complex problem with different facets, and how you approached it?	Logical, methodical, step by step approach Ability to unravel complex issues Ability to remain objective
Facilitation and influential skills	Can you think of an instance where you have had to convince colleagues of the value of project planning?	Ability to work with project team & identify skills. Must be able to influence team to step back and plan project prior to start.
Practical can-do attitude	Can you describe a project during which you come across obstacles? How did you overcome them?	Positive approach Thinking outside box, Problem Solving. Pragmatic approach. Hands-on team member – takes responsibility and moves forward

I'll now leave you with your **Interview Checklist!**

The Look
- ✓ Dark matching suit with light white collared shirt
- ✓ Polished shoes, neat hair, ironed clothes, ditch all excessive jewellery and create an overall good and safe impression

Preparation
- ✓ Read the job advert and/or talk to someone doing the job
- ✓ Do your research on the company website and other sites
- ✓ Know who will be interviewing you. So you know who to ask for and can research them specifically
- ✓ Have your answers prepared for typical interview questions
- ✓ Prepare suitable questions to ask at the end of your interview
- ✓ Print out copies of your CV and make sure you can talk through it in addition to your strengths and achievements

Before you arrive
- ✓ Arrive 15 minutes before the interview; and make sure you have either planned or done the journey
- ✓ Re read the job brief and your research within the hour before the interview to refresh your mind

First impressions last .... SO
- ✓ Create instant impact through a smile, strong hand shake, good eye contact and posture

During the interview
- ✓ Sit up straight, and lean forward – remember body language – no barriers with crossed arms etc.
- ✓ Pause after hearing a question and think carefully about your answers – show that you understand and use examples to help them understand your capabilities

At the end of the interview
- ✓ Ask your questions plus what will happen next
- ✓ Thank them for their time and create a strong final impression – smile, eye contact, strong handshake

Blood, Sweat and Careers

......**Six Steps** to Exceptional Career
Performance

Step **6**

– Evaluate and Refocus

Evaluate and Refocus

The final stage and the most important one is to check you are moving in the right direction.

By now, through engagement with the exercises, I am hoping you have:

- ✓ Evaluated your personal offering outlining your strengths, areas of development and opportunities, key skills and clarified what motivates you.
- ✓ Set BIGG's and Goals
- ✓ Improved your thinking through NLP
- ✓ Put together an "A" Team
- ✓ Worked out a strategy to find hidden job opportunities, work with recruiters and made direct applications to companies you want to work for
- ✓ Written a WIP (work in progress) CV full of achievements
- ✓ Produced a WIP Letter of Application
- ✓ Produced answers to all the potential interview questions and competency based interview questions

But what do you need to do to step up another gear? How can you achieve even more success and which areas did you work on less than others? There is always room for improvement and I think that comes with evaluation, refocus and feedback.

I'm expecting you to also have job offers on the table, but how do you go about deciding if this is what you actually want?

How to Evaluate a Job Offer

Well any job offer should be considered, and considered carefully. If you actually applied for the position, prepared your documents and prepared and engaged in an interview, chances are that at least at one stage this was a role you were interested in?

Although I admit that sometimes the offer that comes through isn't what you expected. In this market it's clear that some employers are offering at the lower end of their scales and thinking "people should be lucky to get an offer". Its an unfortunate mentality and in recruitment I have seen it happen dozens of times. What these employers seem to forget is when the market turns, they will lose the individual who will remain angered at being put in a different situation than when they started the interview process with them.

My advice is – don't undervalue yourself but make sure you consider all elements of the offer before making any decision. I often say this to people who get what they consider to be a very generous offer – it's not just about that short term motivator called money.

The key is to be clear about what you want from the job and the company. Is this position in line with your goals? What will it do for your CV and career development?

I've always worked with professionals who are toying with decisions. Decisions to stay at their firm, take a promotion, take the plunge to a new firm...its not easy. I usually prepare a list of questions to help them make their decision.

If they are in a job already, they will also ask these questions of their current role and firm. Why don't you have a go!

Firstly, refocus on what you are looking for and then see how your current role (if applicable) or your new role matches up to it.

Job Focus Questionnaire:

When asking these questions, prepare your answer and then give the role you are considering a mark out of 10 as to how it compares...

- What industries am I looking for?
- What is the ideal size and structure of my ideal company?
- What mission and values am I looking for?
- What culture am I looking for?
- What work environment suits me best?
- What work life balance do I require?
- What management style do I work well with?
- What kind of people do I want to work with?
- What about teamwork?
- What about my expected level of independence?
- Do I need job/ company security?
- What are my ideal locations?
- What is my ideal role?
- What are my career development expectations?
- What salary and package am I seeking?

There are 15 questions here and so your comparison role could achieve a maximum of 150 points. How did it score?

120 – 150	Consider taking it!
100 – 120	What's your reservation, is it serious enough to forgo this opportunity?
99 or less?	Forget it!

Notes on your opportunities:

"Criticism may not be agreeable, but it is necessary. It fulfils the same function as pain in the human body. It calls attention to an unhealthy state of things."

Winston Churchill

Get some feedback!

Feedback is essential to the growth of any individual or any strategy. How will you know if what you're doing is working without receiving some form of feedback?

Now for the hard part, what would you say if I asked you to go and find out if what you are doing is right and how people perceive you? Would you do it? Are you brave enough?

Oh and what does the little word feedback mean to you?

People don't like the word feedback, especially if it is about themselves as a person or relating to their specific role or activities. It usually makes them nervous and feel it is all about criticism. Anything that is related to a person's performance and that coming under the line of fire is never an exciting moment. But let's think about this logically...

For example: let's say you run a restaurant and the business is well-known and you are a newcomer. The amount of business hasn't changed but regulars seem to be disappearing. You have decided to change a few things in the restaurant to cut costs to improve the overall increase in profits. You have decided to change the seating arrangement to fit more customers into the restaurant, and you have changed the type of seats. You start to notice the lack of returning of your regulars that you have come to know by name and bring in your steady daily income. You decided to make the changes to the restaurant without asking opinions from existing clients or any other person involved.

As time goes on you realise that the changes in the restaurant have caused the regular ladies book club to find an alternative venue as their seating arrangements do not exist anymore with the comfort of the sofa's that you removed. They found the atmosphere comfortable and inviting as well as relaxing which is exactly what they needed.

If you had only gone through the process of getting feedback, you would have found this out earlier without losing customers and then you could have re-evaluated the situation and other areas where you could have cut costs.

Feedback provided the basis for improvement, if you don't know what you are doing wrong how can you fix it or improve on it? It offers the most effective way to development whether it is self development or otherwise. On the other hand if you are doing something well, you also want feedback and encouragement or else you won't know that what you are doing is right and appreciated by others. Think of receiving and giving feedback as it works both ways to help all parties involved to improve on their areas and develop those areas that are excelling.

If you are investing precious time and effort into a strategy or career or goal or whatever it may be, without feedback that time is being wasted. Time is precious, you could have been improving as feedback is received and in doing so have self improved or developed much quicker than without it. You most likely would be 3 steps ahead of yourself and develop yourself 3 times more than you would of. In essence you could have then become a director of a company or started your own business years before you would have if you have received no feedback and no criticism.

'Criticism is something we can avoid easily by saying nothing, doing nothing, and being nothing'
Aristotle

Feedback isn't just about the negatives. How about we change its name and say that there is now no such thing as feedback...only "feedforward"

Does that sound more palatable?

Whatever you want to call it, it is a positive method to improving one self and becoming stronger and even more powerful to advance in your career. In a lot of organisations, people only receive it twice a year when their appraisal comes up. How crazy does that sound? Imagine if you had an employee and wanted to alter their behaviour so they performed better and you were both happier as a result, why wait until their appraisal?

So I want you to take the plunge and go out there and get some. For effective feedback you need people who are going to be honest (and brutal) with you. You also need to agree to take the feedback on board.

So how do you get it?
 - Look all around you and assess where you are, give yourself some honest feedback about what you are doing and how you are performing.
 - Use a coach along the way to guide and assess you regularly
 - Ask for it – from your boss, colleagues, family, friends, suppliers, customers, employees!

Create a form for them to fill in for you if you want!

So how do you take feedback?

- Listen carefully and with an open and clear mind. This will make you more successful. Remember its how they see you, not how you see you!
- Don't interrupt or influence the feedback in any way, let them finish, write it down and say THANK YOU and tell them how it will benefit your development. Nothing more.
- If you unsure about something that has been said, ask for examples to help you understand but make sure you are not doing this to question them.
- Don't get defensive, upset or angry
- Decide what you want to do with the feedback.
- Respond in a positive way and close the meeting in a positive way.
- Get multiples source of feedback!

Exceptional Career Performance

It's not an easy road but with a few adherences to the rules you can get there. So what do you need to watch out for when achieving exceptional career performance?

Firstly, don't forget that there is always somebody listening and somebody watching. Everything you say in your work life is almost like a recording and people don't forget any comments you make. There are no such things as "off the cuff" or "off the record" comments. You need to get this right now if you want to see exceptional career performance.

Chase your passion, not your pension! Don't spend your life doing something you detest, do something you love!

Do something different! If your diary for the next four weeks looks like the last four weeks, what do you expect to happen differently? Stop, change your objectives and make it happen.

Remember the well used titled of the book "winning friends and influencing people"? well this is your next rule. Treat everyone with respect no matter what you think about their ideas. There's a time and a place for feedback and this may not be it.

Learn your skill and train, train and train. Practice makes perfect and there is a clear relationship between competence and success and attitude. Become great at what you do and get all the training you need. This will give you the mind power to surge forward.

Go and get feedback – don't be shy! All the great people have coaches, mentors and of course people who will be truly honest with them. You need to know how you are perceived in order to grow and develop.

Have high expectations for yourself. Set goals and BIGG's and make sure you revisit them every day. It takes moments to re-read a card in your wallet.

Take time to work on the documents for success – have well worked CV's and Profiles – use a career coach if you need to. It's a shrewd investment. Also take note of the secret ways to dig out those opportunities so you are not in the market with everyone else.

Embrace Diversity – we all experience it and this can forge great outcomes if you let it! Everything passes. It's all in your control as to what happens next and its your response plus the event that makes the outcome.

Increase your circle, spending time with the same old contacts and expecting fresh ideas is a mugs game. Get out there and get yourself an "A" Team!

Open yourself up to the unexpected, who knows what, might happen?

Don't be adverse to risk.

Have a plan!

Make your work a calling!

Do things you are good at!

Good luck!

"Would you like me to give you a formula for success?
It's quite simple really. Double your rate of failure."

Thomas J. Watson, founder of IBM

Rewards V Consequences

I remember when I was desperate to put the secrets of successful people down on paper...and yes the reward was always going to be the book at the end of it. But how is that a reward when you are still writing the first chapter. It was really important when I set my goals to make sure I had bite size "mini goals" and after each success was a treat. My partner gave me a trip to Cannes for finishing chapter four! However let me tell you about the first two chapters...

And I guess now is the time to talk about consequences...

I firmly believe that by having a coach you will always stay on track. However I almost fired him when he told me I needed a consequence as well as a reward. The story was I had to come to work in a bikini (and I work on Fleet Street!) if I didn't get the chapters finished by 15th April 2009. He said to me, and I like this view....if your goal is that important to you, accept the consequence because you have nothing to fear if you plan to complete the chapters. I did it.

If you can't reach your goals, your goals will consume you in a negative manner. University of Michigan psychologists have found great evidence that while goals are important, goals can do us a great disservice if they are not flexible.

We make all our decisions with the information we have at the time. But things change. You must update your goals over time as you consider your changing priorities and resources.

28 Days Later

All of this engagement and plan is pointless without action so I am going to ask just one last thing from you.

Commit to Act!

Write down today's date_____

Now tell me what you are prepared to commit to doing in the next 28 days that will make a profound and significant positive impact on your life?

Use your Goals you have already written and breaking them into bite size chunks, write down your commitment AS IF YOUR LIFE DEPENDED ON IT. Next to each bite size goal – write the reward and consequence if you do/do not achieve it.

By the 28th day I will have:

My commitments:	Reward/Consequence:
	My Reward: The Consequence:
	My Reward: The Consequence:
	My Reward: The Consequence:
	My Reward: The Consequence:
	My Reward: The Consequence:
	My Reward: The Consequence:

'Making your mark on the world is hard. If it were easy, everybody would do it. But it's not. It takes patience, it takes commitment, and it comes with plenty of failure along the way. The real test is not whether you avoid this failure, because you won't. it's whether you let it harden or shame you into inaction, or whether you learn from it; whether you choose to persevere'

Barack Obama

What now?

Let's be honest here – only you can answer this one. This is your life and your decision.

And it always has been.

I really hope you think about the goals you have set along with the rewards and consequences of those goals.

Think carefully who can help you in your goals, which people you want to surround yourself with. Who makes up your team? Do you have a coach, a guide, a mentor? Could this benefit you?

I firmly believe a good coach takes people to their destination. Look at anyone with a competitive spirit who seems phenomenal at their game? Talking of games, I guess you all know Tiger Woods? If he is so great on his own, why does he pay Butch Harmon vast amounts of money to be his coach? Butch has never won a Golf Tournament so how could he coach Tiger you may ask....

Butch is a prime example of a great coach and shows how you can still be great without having the hands on experience of reaching the dizzy heights that Tiger has.

However this is where The Chancery Coaching Company is unique. All our coaches have the business acumen, have achieved exceptional career performance and could be an option for you if you feel you need a guide.

If you have enjoyed the book and feel you could benefit further from having a coach to help you in your process, why not work personally with me or any of my hand picked exceptional colleagues?

What do we do at The Chancery Coaching Company?

The Chancery Coaching Company focuses on business professionals who are looking to develop aspects of their life and achieve their full potential. We focus on individuals who are looking to enhance their life, manage and excel in their careers and/or build a business. Our framework is designed to work on the areas that impact your ultimate goals and use techniques to develop these areas.

We specialise in 3 sectors of coaching programmes namely: career, corporate & life coaching...

Our **Career** programmes focus on your specific career growth and path for success whether you are looking to progress in your specific career or change your career entirely.

Our **Corporate** programmes focus on your role and the role of your team in the organisation and its overall goals and objectives - improving your value to the bottom line!

Our **Life** programmes focus on every aspect of life that has an affect both positive and negative on your goals and objectives and in becoming the person you want to be. Here we identify the scope of your success as an individual.

If you are trying to **develop and excel in your career** or embarking on an **entirely new career** path our *Career Coaching Programmes* will give you the knowledge and tools to grow and develop your career as well as equip you with the vision for your entire career path.

Together we will set goals to enable you to excel in the present and work on a brighter future.

Our Bespoke Career Programmes will be set to:

- fully identify your career objectives
- match your skills, experiences and personality profile
- seek the best possible routes for success
- identify all possible setbacks and obstacles
- understand the climate and markets being entered
- plan your entire career path and routes for success
- keep you in line for your set objectives

Our Corporate Coaching Programmes are designed to help you in your current organisation whether as an employee or business owner.

We work on providing a better understanding of the business, your contribution and/or how you can inspire and develop the people in the organisation to reach the business objectives. We also offer valuable business advice for people wishing to start their own business, see it through its incubation and growth stages, and later in assisting in preparing an exit strategy for those wishing to sell or float their business now or in the future.

Go to our website and book yourself a free taster session to see if we are right for you.

www.chancerycoaching.com

You deserve it.
Warm wishes and the best of luck in your search for success!

About the Author

Angela Cahill grew up in the North West of England enjoying the wonderful opportunities and outlook from having a Scottish Mother and Kuwaiti Father.

Interestingly her career path started extremely early on having a desire for the business world at the tender age of 16. Angela was the youngest person to work and take weekend charge of a high profile Estate Agency, was hired by the Government at 18 for a summer program and was quickly promoted to management with a leading franchise organisation. Along with fitting in a University Degree of course!

At 21 and armed with a BA Hons in Marketing, Angela enjoyed a stint with a National News and Media organisation before facing the obvious. Her love of all things career based. Angela took the role of an Executive Recruiter and Headhunter for one of the largest recruitment firms in the world. After enjoying a record breaking rise up the career ladder, she went on to start her own business at the age of 27.

Angela now runs three successful businesses, recently went back to night school to study law, takes on Headhunting Assignments for a handful of her favourite clients, is a regular speaker on Career Management and a Corporate and Career Coach.

She believes her success is down the three things: Living each day as if it's your last, knowing and achieving your dreams and having enormous amounts of fun!

For a free coaching taster session go to:

www.chancerycoaching.com

To buy copies of this book, go to:

www.bloodsweatandcareers.com